WHAT WE'RE DOING TO STAY AFLOAT

KARIN COPE

POTTERSFIELD PRESS, LAWRENCETOWN BEACH, NOVA SCOTIA, CANADA

Library and Archives Canada Cataloguing in Publication

Cope, Karin, 1964-, author
        What we're doing to stay afloat : poems / Karin Cope.
ISBN 978-1-897426-75-3 (paperback)
        I. Title.
PS8605.O6792W53 2015   C811'.6   C2015-904110-4

Cover photo: Paulette Phillips. Video still from Floating House, 2002.

Cover concept: Raven Davis

Cover design: Gail LeBlanc

We acknowledge the financial support of the Government of Canada through the Canada Book Fund for our publishing activities. We acknowledge the support of the Canada Council for the Arts. Nous remercions le Conseil des arts du Canada de son soutien. Pottersfield Press recognizes the support of the Province of Nova Scotia We are pleased to work in partnership with the Province of Nova Scotia to develop and promote our creative industries for the benefit of all Nova Scotians.

Pottersfield Press
83 Leslie Road
East Lawrencetown, Nova Scotia, Canada, B2Z 1P8
Website: www.PottersfieldPress.com
To order, phone 1-800-NIMBUS9 (1-800-646-2879) www.nimbus.ns.ca

Printed in Canada

For my parents,
Jim and Marcia Cope,
who read aloud daily,
mixing poetry with prayer

Contents

3.

Little thunderclaps: sonatinas of love and night

4.

What we're doing to stay afloat

5.

Blind / Closely watched tides

A poem about

"Can we put in orders, can we be patrons?
I would like a poem about –
where was the line I
crossed but didn't notice? Your
first botany notebook.
Hot taste of homemade raspberry
pie; picking berries in the
summer sun. How
rocks get old. The hum
ming of Glenn Gould. World in
black and white. Molecules of
chocolate.
Do we all have a wall of
prayer? Where?"

1.

Shouting in the dark

A special name for careless is caress.
– Gertrude Stein, "A Sonatina Followed by Another"

The daily disaster

odd couple   one fat   one thin
living in the wild
— but which is which

they have two dogs
one can only run (it cannot walk)
the other can only walk (it cannot run)

five cars
one driver's license
a riding horse that bucks and rears

they've given it a goat then taken it back
afraid the horse will kick
bought ducks instead and a plastic pool

the days pass
you think something will happen but it never does
one is sick then the other

this year tomatoes won't flower
spiders web the grass
the well dries   the basement floods

roof tiles crack   they replace them
mow the grass
plant marigolds

drink too much
cease altogether
take it up again

gain five pounds lose two
vow to give up sugar and cigarettes
twist an ankle break a back

the dogs run off, don't return
tides go up tides go down
backhoe digs a horse-sized grave

Of want and wit born

Hunger and Misery live side by side, no longer speaking
in their too big house.
In the cold blue light in the stark white bath (unheated),
toothpaste: no other creams.
They've tied a plastic tube
to the faucet to force the water down. In the corner,
kneepads. At the appointed hour, Hunger sings his sins
amid the tiles: how heart and eyes and want
have strayed. That big old house leaks
heat; cold ices windows; they wear their coats
at table. Come night, they watch *Survivor*; Misery
crochets reruns; wool tangles in her lap. Who said love
was born of want and wit knew this:
how elaborate, how burnished their celebrations.

Real estate speculation
(death of a painter)

I.
You never liked to be cold.

As soon as you died they took your things away.
(Yuppies' trumpet.)

Sheer curtains double beds pink sheets button hassocks
braided rugs faded jeans a peasant dress sensible shoes
threadbare towels linen smocks flowing scarves
– that infamous panama hat! –
rubber boots broken umbrellas barn jackets scuffed mules
bunny slippers your
lace up boots – all are gone:
Estate Sale.

They boxed your paintings – six to the local museum –
then sold your hordes of paint
on craigslist,
rolls and cans of brushes bolts of canvas gessoed panels
stretchers frames boxes buckets of turpentine pencils
pastels and rulers glass belayers pliers
hammers saws nails shears
– everything but the chalkboard where you used to plan
(wipe errors easily away!).
It's all that's left in the studio.
(Gestalts and spectral surfaces buried here.)

When the plants died – who came to water them? Your executors?
She's in Ontario, he's in Calgary – they tipped them out at the edge of
the drive and stacked the pots
beneath the stairs. Lumps of dry earth and brittle leaves.
(Chester L Stump Crust has joined a men's group.)

They can't wait to sell the house.

II.
Anyone can see what they've missed –
Gestalts and spectral surfaces buried here –
Yuppies' trumpet scribbled on the wall,
a mouldering rind of cheese in the fridge.
There's the half empty jug of orange juice a frozen chicken an open tin
of salmon-flavoured cat food – where is your kitty now? –
and that crude icon painted by Fred Insmith. You bought it to encourage
him – the title itself worth something:
Chester L Stump Crust has joined a men's group.
Silly junk of carmined wood propped on the ledge beside the spare key.

Your fingerprints span the doorframe
a rainbow patter on the thermostat;
they're your last ghostly painting there on the wall:

you never liked to be cold.

Do we know what we see?

Rain overnight. Wet spatters the windows in howling wind.
Insomniac, I drop logs on the fire, scribble notes
in the dark, wake in fog. Now
sunshine. Sharp shadows cross the lawn, grass
imperceptibly greening. Everything changes. Nothing
does. Do we know what we see?
Afternoon. A bat drops on the porch floor
trembling, mouse brown thing, with
tiny feet, awkward in the light.
I watch it breathing – *Is it sick? Is it rabid?* –
carry it to a rock by the pond. It watches
me. Sun shines through flared wings. Bat bares
its teeth, bites on a thorn: small
mouth blooms rose red.

Pocket full of rusty nails

On the other side of
grocery lists & balls of lint &
six sharp stones,
on the other side of *tell me who is*
talking who is singing why she says
the buzzing in my head &
a pocket full of rusty nails,
if ever, someday,
despite poor eyesight and mouldy pears,
somewhere,
some other mouthful,
(not this one)
will taste round & full like
clear blue air.

Things gone wrong

two men   one night   a drink   a fight
over a woman? maybe a dog

(they were friends since second grade)

Piper wrestles Tek to the ground behind his truck   ties him to the hitch
for a lark   or a lesson   he pulls him   up the road

the rope twists   Tek tries to run behind can't keep up   sways
          falls hard   cracks his teeth
rivulets of stone rake his pretty face   twenty feet of gravel rub him raw

cops put Piper in handcuffs   charges   counter charges   court dates
          lawyers
jail time   more for belligerence than crime

five years later looks like they've kissed and made up   wives now and
          kids
saddled   they laugh

one fall they think they'll go deer hunting grease up the guns head into
          the trees
side by side they startle   four deer graze a clearing   the deer scatter so
          do the men

scramble through scrub over rock up hill the day a flurry of breath steam
          brown
flickering motion

Tek stops to tie his shoe sees a flash of brown fires red report echoes in
     grey rock oh
his aim is true and   Piper   down shot to the head   dead

trembling Tek lifts the body carries his awful burden over   another
threshold

prison he writes Piper's wife *if they'd still hang a guilty man I'd*
she plots her own revenge

soul as stinking as his teeth, the bugger beading prayers with the
children she promises *where he's going no moon will shine*

ten years run to fifteen Tek appears his slicked back hair his stiff
     cleaned jeans his
careful prison words she plugs her ears gets her gun   Tek

down   who could know there would be so much blood   she'll never
     wash it
out

when the cops come she runs   grandbaby sleeps in the crib
     too late
another one down before

the law   law says
by the time we get to them, they're on their tenth bad decision

Too windy for the birds

Backlit clouds of morning blare.
Behind huddled islands, it's
raining out to sea.

Silver spray flies,
wets dark and stunted trees –
too windy for the birds.

That rock in the bay looks like a boat again:
lone fisherman bound home and

forever missing shore.

Hurt birds
(on the politics of blame)

Listen, another dream. Small birds are fluttering
in my hands. They are little, like finches, but blue, rust and cream. Not
anything like swallows. We stand by the window in some
private study; thick volumes suck every sound and
I think my ears are ringing. It is cold; it must be
winter. Bare branches scratch the glass. I settle
little birds on a table; they gather in a huddle. They are
hurt. I've been plucking feathers from their
wings; I don't know why I do it.
I wake to the cat (that incubus)
asleep on my chest. What do you think: could she
enwrap me, could she make me dream her dreams?
Wait. Let me name my own cruelty;
I should not blame the cat.

The house is on fire

prose is a house
poetry a man in flames running quite fast through it
Anne Carson, *Red Doc*

Try a morning when the dog barks you up:
hungry geese are on the lawn.
Unmoored ice shards and founders,
every grass blade dead and yellow.
How long must we
wait for the season to shift?
Slow spring, the kid
at the fuel stop says. While gas guzzles,
snow gathers on the windscreen.
You speed off, late for dinner.
Why is poetry an emergency?
Our hearts knock
against a stubborn world. Inside,
forever, the house is on fire.

When in another's house

1. Let sleeping dogs lie.

2. Resist the urge to run to the kitchen, to pour a bowl of bran buds and milk.

3. Try to keep the freezer door closed. Do not steal frozen steaks.

4. As for the corner where they keep the broom: don't hide there.

5. Stop refolding mussed linens,

6. and measuring out the laundry soap.

7. If you must climb into a closet, then go ahead! Try on some shoes!

8. Ask, if you want to borrow a coat, a dress, a pair of gloves.

9. Try not to leave hair in another's brush.

10. And if you will drink more, don't hide your bourbon under the bed.

Did you think I wouldn't find the glass?

2.

At the ice edge

I see now that saints are needed.
– Alice Notley, "Desert Poems"

If you had wings

If you had wings, what would you do with them?

I would fly out to the ice edge and see who fishes
there; what the hooded mergansers scoop, which
silver fingerling the loons prefer. I would watch snow melt
in the sea. I would fly to the hilltop where the sun bounds up
and swoop over the islands: High, Baptiste and Broken Back,
Ship, Goose, Black Duck, the Halibuts, the Birds,
Softwood, Hardwood, Deadman, Beaver,
Pumpkin, Horse and Flag. I'd stop at the Harbour Islands and sit
by an otter, watch the tide come in.
Later the eagle and I would meet in an updraft;
I'd stare her down:
> *my current, my space; I'm here: don't bother me. Go
> find your own air.*
That settled, I would carry on, whispering, like prayer.

Unfreeze
(not quite a valentine)

What we did and would and could
What we should
What we did not and why
Which we couldn't
What she said
What I did
How some words flick open, slip slick steel beneath the bone
How others encyst and grow tumorous, stopping up the lungs
How what was fluid became solid
How the sea was covered in ice and the rain needled down, encasing cars
        in brittleness
How a gesture incompleted never –
How stillness shattered
How the leg of a chair flung down
bounces   and does not
break

In Desolation Sound
(Bathsheba's poem)

Sharp rattle of relief:
rain patters in a dry place, gives a sense
of letting go. – Or sudden terror:
the sodden suck, the lack of
air, as if you're drowning.
Too much, too soon, a flood
of missing: blasted. Echoless. O grief.
Rain drums against taut canvas
sighs joy and lamentation, signs
pinpricks heart's ease fur furrows ear flaps dog's paws
sings the scent of grass upon her feet.
We tumble into fog into
seal's slap and wolfish wail, blind
to what they see or know. So near,
so far; too late to bring you home.

Sounds of things you cannot hear

Snow falling on a doe's nose;
twitch of the hairs that line her ears; how
our nervous eyebeams cross and stutter; when
spindrift flurries smash and drop.

Otter prints at the water's edge;
taste of grass beneath the pines;
flank's quiver, heart's thump, and the
sudden savour of coyote paws.

Hunger marches across the pond, by
rabbit trails and pheasant scratchings,
crouches near the flattened rushes, where
come night, some creature sleeps.

Somewhere a doe is always watching –
fluttering startle, tail flicker, flattened grass and trampled snow.

At the ice edge

At the ice edge

pain

and rough slabs of poetry.

3.

Little thunderclaps: sonatinas of love and night

Are you teasing us, dark Night?
What're you holding under your cloak?
– Novalis, *Hymns to the Night*, trans. Dick Higgins

When last I died

When did you last die?
Last night, three hours before the moon set. And then I woke again.

What gets you out of bed in the morning?
The thought of getting back into it at night. And sometimes a eucalyptus
bath. Coffee keeps me up, as do endless lists of tasks. I cross one
off; the day adds three. Or five, or ten. This is why I die every
night; it's a way of resetting the clock. Alas, the list survives.

What became of your childhood dreams?
All I remember is nightmares from which I am glad to have awakened.

What sets you apart from everyone else?
Nothing. I wear others' castoffs, and can hardly remember a new pair of
shoes. In any case, I will surely fit into another pair someone else has
tossed aside.

What is missing from your life?
Nothing and then everything and then nothing again, so that I tumble
into a quandry without top or bottom.

Do you think that everyone can be an artist?
Of course. Everyone but myself, naturally. Which is why I must make
such an effort to insist that I too might someday think of myself
this way. Just not yet.

Where do you come from?
I grew up in a flat place south of this one, a thousand miles from the sea.
The lights of the city blocked out the stars, and I thought that the
endless roar of the traffic was the sound of the void.
I was, perhaps, right about that.

Do you find your lot an enviable one?
I have no truck with envy, although desire is everything. Can you desire a
lot? Yes, I do.

What have you given up?
Lent. Small purchases. And often, hope.

What do you do with your money?
I put it into a household account and there it disappears. I am not sad
about this; what else should I do with my money?

What household task gives you the most trouble?
I hate vacuuming, spot removal, scrubbing the bathtub and fixing others'
computers. Correcting grammar mistakes. Yet I seem to be
expert in all of these things.

What are your favourite pleasures?
You really think I'm going to tell you? Summer. Peaches. The scent of
dogs' paws. In another life I might have been a dancer.

What would you like to receive for your birthday?
All of the poems of CD Wright, Pablo Neruda and César Vallejo. A really
sturdy tripod. A new pair of shoes. Or a swimming pool; the sea
is really too cold for sport these days.

Cite three living artists whom you detest.
Artists? I can't think of one. But politicians, managers, corporate
kleptocrats? May evil befall the lot of them, they who are the
scourge that scours us. You want me to name them? Ayy, where
do I begin? Just pick up the newspaper, pluck names from the
front page.

What do you stick up for?
Virtually everyone else.

What are you capable of refusing?
Butter. Sugar. Cream. A ride. I wish I were capable of refusing stupidity,
but sometimes I tumble into it and cannot climb out.

What is the most fragile part of your body?
My feet. Or perhaps my breath. This is why I did not become a dancer,
although I still long for such precise athleticism. Words rarely
fail me, but my body lumbers; it is less reliable than it used to be.

What has love made you capable of doing?
Love has made me capable of hatred. Of rage, of going to battle. Strange
perhaps, because the opposite is not true – rage and hatred don't
make me capable of love.

What do other people reproach you for?
Unfinished projects. Belatedness. Abstraction. Absence. Falling down
when I should be standing up. Loving the wrong things. And
they are right. I, too, reproach myself for these failings, among
others.

What does art do for you?
Sometimes it's the only door to hope. Without it, I don't think much of
us.

Write your epitaph.
Wait, that's not a question. I would prefer not to. Not yet, even if I
am always dying. See? Another unfinished project. A belated
requiem. Let us sing.

In what form would you like to return?
I would be a winged thing, fleet of foot: nimble, pirouetting, light of
heart, ripe and tender as a peach in July.

Observations on ice

Clouds always tell a true story ... one ... difficult to read.
Ralph Abercromby,
"Suggestions for an International
Nomenclature of Clouds," 1887

Saturday	Water Pools in Dead Grass
Sunday	A Scattering of Snow
Monday	Rain Falls on Ice
Tuesday	Ice Rots and Gutters
Wednesday	The Sea is a Lung
Thursday	Suddenly Sun Flashes
Friday	Every Solid Soon Founders

Winter galls us

Who can bear how winter clings and stops us
at the root? Colour is something memory finds,
a gap, an aching loss
in a world awash in weeviling greys and
stinging damp: mould's heaven, not ours.
We long for sun or a meteor shower,
for a sudden pressing bud, or
the arcs and angles of a swallow's flight.
Who could be content with last year's apples,
or the bitter dregs of yesterday's tea?
Leftover news in a snow-darkened sky.
Like business-as-usual, winter galls us, excoriates hope.
Who lives without promise of ripeness, without
a burst of juice between the teeth?

Letters in the dark

Comes night. Name a tongue who licks your ear;
unpaint the winging of your heart;
spell the shelter which hides its shadow;
what the glass would see if it had eyes;
who let the lamp beam blare and sound;
who told the saddest lie;
who threw the fourteenth stone;
who faltered in the ditch;
who danced with flute and hammer;
who tongued the holy bread;
who swept blind ash into a cup;
who drank your studied dregs;
who wept and splashed and shunned the shore;
who slept when it was light.

Sing summer morning

having wakened early · today we rise late
   this may take some time

already clouds cover up the sky
   – what kind of clouds?
   – stratus clouds they lie in layers like a moisture napoleon

later on meaning later tonight maybe tomorrow
it will rain
   this may take some time

lines of current wind river runs through it I mean the calm sea
just there right in front of us a shimmering wide band and no bank to
sit on

then the birds the birds the birds
they sing hour upon hour since four a.m.

   they take their time everything is time
   keeping time counting it taking its measure

but I haven't been listening
because I've been sleeping which is to say wasting which is to say losing

   time

the way people can
tumbled in dream in memory biting a lush sun-ripened peach

fuzz in my teeth your ·
juice bathes my chin

The whales came again last night

The whales came again last night
bumping up against the hull, gurgling
at the through-holes, rocking gently rocking. They
began to sing to us – damp fingers
on the mouths of goblets, slip-stick crystal music,
pure ether knitting voices in the night.
I dreamed we'd seen them singing, those after –
midnight whales, oddly jointed giants
with crayon-coloured skins, aquamarine
and rusty red. In my dream,
in the waking world, no one cared what
we had seen. They went about their daily
lives, pumping gas, sweeping up, calculating.
But we had heard the whales sing.

No longer hiring

Today, the end of something.

It comes abruptly;
in thirty seconds I am shuddered elsewhere.
I arrive in a place without paving, without shoulder or roundabout.
        Wheels are no use here –
From this point: water.

And here's the strange thing:
I am giddy with relief. I must remember this,
today the first day warm enough to stop on the street and
        turn your face to the light –
        the sun alone ignites happiness.

Here's another thing: every person in the city's out, walking a dog;
three punk rock teens feed their apple to a starling.
Generosity is everywhere, and always surprising.

Look at it!
The joy will outlast summer!

Lost last days of summer

Dry heat in golden light. Dusty
roads. Cornsilk and warm
tomatoes. Dogs ride in
truckbeds, tongues
lolling. Stones in your shoes and
the sweet smell of water, forest
shadow, red cedar. Green moss
and blackberry bramble, sweet slick afternoon.
Three pirates – and one damp dog –
roll down the dock, leap and scatter.
Dog barks. *Do it again.*
Watch me! I can do a handstand!
Dive deep, dive down, find what you can:
stopwatch, rusty spike, fish shadow, cuttlebone.

Red boat haiku

Thin skim of sea ice –
the small red boat rocks at dock,
tethered to summer.

Flexible dates

Mind reading and mentalism. Camera gear!
Free psychic reader, 30 years. (*I'm glad you're*
gone, I wish I had gone with you) Raw food. Garden party.
Thursday afternoon in the pet
store. You in your motorcycle jacket
looking at the fish. (*Rebecca and I*
miss you) Me, talking to the bored bird. I thought we
had a moment (*I miss everything about you*) in
the hyperbaric chamber. Belly dancing. (*When the*
time is right) You must speak Swiss
German. Have own platinum
dolls. Flexible dates. August 14,
2-5 pm. (*You know who you are, you were –   Bowling.*) Come
home now the dog is waiting.

4.

What we're doing to stay afloat

"Be wary of the way you think things look."
– Dee Vadnais

What we're doing to stay afloat

We've hired a plumber to saw the top shelves from the library.

We've changed our motto:
A good foundation is all anyone needs or
The rest will grow back.

Meanwhile, in the elevator shaft,
one who was supposed to fix the roof knits in the dark.

He calls it a sweater, but it has neither armholes nor space for the head.
As for the body that will wear it:
"A garment is to live in," he says.

Some insist he's composing our shroud,
but others call it a *bridal veil* or
a roadmap, or even
an elevator.

We knock on the walls,
drop letters and petitions into the hole,
send a cat through a gap in the brick to unravel the garment by night.

No one will say it,
but she seems to be neglecting her duties.
I too have been wakened by mice burrowing in my navel.

A secret, more radical sect among us believe the garment will catch the
      wind.
Someday soon.
Our knitter will drift up from the shaft and rise into ether.

Who will need fifteen staircases then?

They call the garment *a flight plan*,
which in our language means
manifest or sometimes *chequebook*
or *the dog must have his supper*
or *I'm sorry there is no more soup.*

It's no wonder we're confused.

What to do?

The carpenter drills holes in all the pipes:
messages in Braille for our blind knitter.
Little Fountains, he calls them.

It's a critical success:
"If you can't fly, try swimming."
We like his work so much we've ordered up
another building.

With any luck, we'll soon be underwater.
Singing.

Oh that will be the day;
all our worries will be over then.

Anything could happen

the air this morning smells blue it is pure and clear like the sea twisted
    this way and that by faraway airs
robins on the grass   a foghorn out of order toots in clear sun
cirrus streaks flutter ragged flags over eastern islands (nothing but water
    from here to Spain)
lilies not yet but almost blooming their lily blues scent slides into yellow
    and blue day
blues day jaune with birdsong   with orange light   with robin breast
    with newly stacked wood (oh we are so proud so timely so neatly
    done before the mud comes)
meanwhile on the porch paint is peeling revealing bad taste in golds and
    browns
mown grass dries in yellow drifts on the lawn pale scent of hay tumbles

hear now the sparrow's song the swallow's arc and chatter its
looping flight the distant echo of birdsong in the acres of forest hills
wind blows the hollowed corpse of a fly across the floorboards
and even this is beautiful an insect again airborne after death
we could wish for fates equally fine   (postmortem elevation   an
    observing eye)

funereal screel of a rusty pulley dumps a lobsterman's catch onto the
dock a dirge a moan a pitiable squeal   we'll soon boil brown
lobsters red

nothing ever stays the –
even the dead   transmute

In the company of painters

i.
How to illustrate the day.
Since I'm not a painter but a poet, I'll call it *In the Company of Painters*,
or
what I've heard them say. Phrases like
(*Gather your whites*) or
where do your silences fall? Who cannot love
the names of colours, let us repeat them (*Blue Phtalo, Venetian Red,
Burnt Sienna*). Unlike poets, when you're a painter you're not painting
names (*Viridian Green, Raw Umber*). I guess we're all spreading
shadows, picking out
ocular vibrations. They quote
Van Gogh's letters to Theo (*Don't scatter your darks*)
and Cézanne's enigmas (*Let your colours answer each to the other*).
Good advice if you can listen.

If I were a painter, I would put Picasso's line in: *Each of us, a colony
        entire.*
To register how curious, how changeable the heart.

If I were a painter, what difference would it make? Would I see
        something else, would the world go strange?

*Today, as we were sailing to Isla Coronados,
we passed through broad bands of orange-hued current:
suddenly, blue sea red-veined and leaking.*

ii.
We watched Dee paint in San Juanico. We sat on a stony beach, in
    ceaseless heat. The mountains shimmered.

No blue for a sky; this
surprised me.

More advice from painters (*Things don't look the way you think they
    should*).

If I tried could I learn would I see

raw sienna skies yellowed glare of torrid sun   eyes and hills
gone incandescent   viridian or
pink?

Autumn arrives (and you would say)

Sunday
And you would say
grasses golden in the light

Wednesday
And you would say
leaves and flowers gather in my cup

Thursday
And you would say
houses darken in the rain

Friday
And you would say
sky bruised blue above the sea

Saturday
And you would say
scent of woodsmoke on the road

Another Saturday
And you would say
mornings I passed them huddled in their coats

Sunday
And you would say
snap of lightning in the night

Thursday
And you would say
ice rimes the wall

Saturday
And you would say
the furnace rattles

Wednesday
And you would say
snow clings to window ledges

Given wind (a meditation on time)

In autumn the orchard clings to its fruit. A month
passes. More. The wind,
and we, rattle the branches; some
apples fall. At dusk deer graze
amid the trees. More apples
drop. Crows stake claim as we would, and
haul or hole the fruit.
Rain and wind fell more
fodder; deer print, deer scent; they come
and go. Someone nuzzles the bark.
Early November. A single apple
clings to the tree:
shriveled, rotting, impossibly
stubborn.

Nothing lasts

Bare branches sweep the sky
sunlight scatters shadow
the radio speaks of snow.

Yellow coltsfoot splits grey stone
blasted wood rots and slivers, the old shed
cants and tumbles.

Nothing stays; nothing lasts;

not
this cold, not
this wind, not

that streak of cloud.

What is not seen

Warmer this week and we are buried in fog;
the sea, when you can see it, stone smooth grey.

When we wake, the sound of rain.
Is it really raining or is that fogwater?

It gathers in the gutters;
it runs down the roof, dribbles in the walls.

Fog so thick it blinds you;
air so damp, matches won't strike.

Friends come to visit.
We sit in the dark, tongues flickering. They talk

about a film their cats were in: 12
house cats together on a country jaunt.

*What kind of nut would put a dozen
cats in a car?* My cat is mesmerized

by birds chirping in the deadwood,
but she won't get her feet wet.

Sun comes and goes like emotion, feelings linger
in damp green light.

Look how it's always high tide these days;
that's global warming for you.

Hearts ease bleeding heart garden glove *oh look
here come the lilacs.* Damn it's raining again

and the house is leaking cats huddle in darkness and Scarlatti cantatas
(water drips on the speakers).

Lay me down on porcupine droppings and sing
of northern lights. We've gone invisible tonight.

Antics of several species lately observed on Vancouver Island

i

Everything aggregates
in the spring:
boats docks anenomes
blossoms shades of blue and
shades of green
starfish gather under pilings
lines tangle on decks and wharves
otter paws trail water
from cedar board
to cedar board.

ii

Everything proliferates
in the spring:
jackstand bicycle wheelbarrow
waste diesel waste oil new signs
white paint rowing punt
house for sale wave upon wave
of refracted sun.

iii

Everything is prodigal
in the spring.
Like Feather Dusters (subclass *sedentaria*), but
profligate,
wavering heads full of wanderlust,
we root ourselves in water
grit and light. We hymn
the margin,
love the strand.

Night-dark day

Night-
dark day,
dismal drizzle
crying gulls. One boat plows
through mist, hauls weighted
traps, throws star-
fish back.

I am thinking of my mother

I am
thinking of my
mother sliding through some
dappled light, on her way to
market.

She circles
by the pond, she
gathers in her doubt; she
listens to the frogs sing: birth; muck;
breath; hope.

5.

Blind / Closely watched tides

"I could never live where the tides don't go in and out."
– Elsie Blackie, Grand Manan Island

On some differences in style

I.
Canadian

      Spare voices of arctic landscape scoured
clean of colour by the howling blast.
Wind that trims away every stripling, eats
bark from trees, polishes
snow to steel, leaves
no moss.

      Out here we survive
on lichens
grey whorls tightly clinging
                    to rock.

Poetic

      Build no fires
Let no searing tongues leap up
to the night sky. (Let nothing be
visible
anywhere on the plain.)

Advice

      (Cover is everything.)

II. Rules for American Poetry

1. Add every word you know. Add extra locutions too!
2. Make it jump! Make it jazz! Make it jangle, rumble, rattle and rhyme.
3. A little chili, let it sizzle, fry some fat, do add salt.
4. Bite down hard.
5. Let crumbs fly.
6. If the sun is high, don't bother with a hat.

April Sunday morning / moods in falling snow

Risen from the blindness of sleeping to dull light of morning.
Shadows flare and blur. When I find my glasses: sudden sharp edges.
Snowflakes gather in clusters, bomb by the windows –
Oh why get up; let me close my eyes.
But the dog wants breakfast and the fire must be lit, so I stand up.
Waves swarm the harbour, rush in to land:
this battle will be lost. Gritty foam scatters on the beach,
clings to stone, tumbles end over end.
Lately I'm hearing voices as if
the radio's half un-plugged.
There's this song that someone is singing
in a language I can't understand.
In the newspaper, rows of North Korean children hold red scarves.
No one mentions hunger, just *missiles, thermonuclear threat, diplomatic
        talks.*
Crows cackle in the snow, and the sparrows do not sing.

Suddenly sparrows

Suddenly sparrows and
constant singing.
They begin before sunrise.

Cluster of eiders at the point.
Geese root in dead grasses,
and the pheasants are silly.

Yesterday lobster boats launched,
traps tower up the dock:
wakes lop onshore.

Muddy boots and earthy scent,
racing ditchwater clatter:

still no frogs.

Blue odour of iodine

Strange and complicated morning. Skim of ice
calms the sea; sudden colour scours your eyes.
Bright light white heat flood the house.
Throw open the windows! Fling wide the door!
Flash of kingfisher wing and peaked blue crest
(*you're back! we're so glad to see you!*). Sparrows sing.
Scent of –   open water. Salt, of course. Blue
odour of iodine, knotted rotting bladderwrack,
sun-warmed grey stone steeped in cold mud:
each element bound to its proximate. Life
on the strand, lived at an edge, wind-tumbled,
cloud-driven. Unstable. Chance-riven.
What peculiar mercy makes us forget that
with heat, comes fog?

Blind

i.

Can your eyes get stuck in near focus? I should know
I'm blind.

No, not blind. They call that myopia, from the Greek, near-sighted.

Anything more than a foot from my face blurs; at greater distances, things disappear.

Do you believe in the power of prayer? God please let the wind come up
and blow this fog away.

Yes or no do you believe I said wait and see if it's

Armageddon or not.

How can I cut the grass when it's always so wet? Even the vegetables rot
on the vine. You mean grapes. I mean lettuce please pass the salt.

How can you notice anything when you can't see?

I mean, how can you think?

More than six trillion sold; two million incarcerated.

What have we done? Oh what have we wrought?

Trying to divine the true meaning and implications for the future – Deflation, Inflation,
Devaluation, Armageddon. It makes a difference which it is.

I stay awake at night just thinking about it but what can you do? Save us
now and at the end of our days amen.

The cat's so soft.

Turn over now and go to sleep come here, I'll hold you.

Yes but what if this is the end of our days?

What does Armageddon mean? I mean literally.

The last battle. You won't see it coming. We live and die as if in fog.

We do anyway. Please I'm scared. I can't see anything. High or low

beams it doesn't matter. Hurry up now and turn off the light.

I'm cold. What was that you said about the end

of days. Don't leave me please in this awful night. I am drowning.

The empire's crumbling. Wait, don't close the window

I can't breathe if you do. But I thought you said you were cold. Hurry up

now. Get into bed.

ii.

More than a trillion gone overnight and still we are

counting. Unlike hamburgers

dollars aren't eaten one at a time. What are we going to do?

Same as always. Go to sleep wake up eat dream think. Yes but

the world is changing, we'll be drowned in the rush.

That could happen. Think of global warming. Will this fog

ever lift?

68

First light. I hear birds chirping but I cannot see

them. Par for the course. Stretch out your arm; your fingers are lost

in the mist. We set out in the fog to fetch her. We rowed and rowed until a boat

rose

from the gloom. It was our boat! We got back aboard and hoped she would wait.

But I know they will come after me, they won't forget me. We figured we were lucky not

to get lost in this soup. No one would know.

You think you know but you don't. You're disoriented. He makes the best ice cream.

Did you try the cherry chip? No the green tea. Because you just can't see.

It's not the foresight that matters so much as the insight, still a little clearing

would be nice.

I know they'll come for me. Blow north wind blow so we can see again.

Presbyopia, old man, that's when you lose it in both directions. If it couldn't be fixed she'd be legally blind.

My sister's worse. That's because

none of you want to see what's going on. The bugs are terrible aren't they?

Do we always have mosquitoes this early in the year? The tide is higher and higher.

It's eating the shore. How many trees fell this year?

That's what you call global warming. Hurry come to bed now,

my feet are cold.

iii.

We are always in the fog.

What we can't see bears down upon us.

Myopia, Presbyopia, if *ope* means hole, *ops* means eye my damaged eye.

The cat sees the birds and wants to go outside

but doesn't want to get her feet wet.

Hold on now and don't let go stay like this; we'll get through

Armageddon. Came up over the blind crest

and she was on the wrong side of the line at the last minute I swerved

you never know what will happen keep a look out I'm so sorry she said

I can't see.

When first you set out

When first you set out, your feet don't know where the road will go,
or how. The head thinks it knows, but it does not.
Who can explain our fragility? Or the beauty of ice in a broken space?
It befalls us: as necessary, as ordinary, as uncomfortable as prayer.
What is the meaning of life?
Why are some days so full of light?
For those who go on living,
there is no experience without an undergoing.
Lightning struck, we stagger, try
to be like the tree that groaning, still stands. Noble beyond
measure. Beautiful in every cracked and shattered limb.
Who cares about perfection? I want to learn
from those who carry on, blind as we all are,
but abiding, open-hearted.

Notes

A poem about leans upon the contents of a letter from Marie-Therese Blanc, and is dedicated to her.

The phrase "**born of Want and Wit**" references an account of the origins of love in Plato's *Symposium*.

All of the italicized phrases and many of the specific details in **Real estate speculation** were found in a house for sale on Vancouver Island in 2011.

I owe the last line of **Things gone wrong** to Chris Stockard, hemispheric sailor and former Alaska State Trooper.

Sources of **If you had wings** include Susan Stewart's dialogue poem, "Wings," the names of the islands in the Bay of Isles on the Eastern Shore of Nova Scotia, and a story told by Ken Cheslock about piloting a glider in the updrafts off the Fundy shore.

In Desolation Sound remembers our black Lab, Bathsheba, who died suddenly of a burst tumour in her lungs while we were sailing in British Columbia.

Sounds of things you cannot hear was suggested by a story found in Richard Louv's *Last Child in the Woods* (2008). In explaining "why the young (and the rest of us) need nature," and what he means by "coming to our senses," Louv recounts a game played by Janet Fout, an environmental activist, with her daughter Julia. "As they wandered through the woods, they would listen for 'the sounds they could not hear': "sap rising, snowflakes forming and falling ... dew on the grass, a seed germinating, an earthworm moving through the soil" (pp. 76-77).

I owe the phrase "rough slabs of poetry" in **At the ice edge** to Jack Wong.

The questions in **When last I died** were proposed by French artist Sophie Calle at the end of an article in which she was interviewed in "Sophie Calle: Interview." *Frieze Magazine.* http://www.frieze.com/issue/article/sophie_calle/

The phrase "what the glass would see if it had eyes" in **Letters in the dark** is by George Oppen.

We first heard the sounds I describe in **The whales came again last night** while anchored in Khutze Inlet, in northern B.C.

No longer hiring ends by quoting two lines from Robin Blaser's 1959 poem "Quitting a Job": "Look at it! The joy will outlast summer!"

Lost last days of summer details life on Texada Island, B.C., in August.

Flexible dates was composed entirely from words lifted from the back pages of a June 2009 issue of *The Coast*, a free weekly newspaper distributed in Halifax, Nova Scotia.

What we're doing to stay afloat is dedicated to the students and staff at the Nova Scotia College of Art and Design University (and every other public institution), who continue to struggle through the logical absurdities of bureaucratic and corporate "rationalization" and the imposition of contradictory rhetorics of austerity.

In the company of painters is dedicated to Dee Vadnais, with enormous thanks for the excitement of her "extreme painting" lessons in the Sea of Cortez.

Nothing lasts owes the phrasing "speaks of snow" to the lively speech of our friend and Eastern Shore neighbour, Ramey Munroe.

What is not seen is dedicated to Danica Meredith and Matt Bergbusch; it relies on a story they recounted one foggy evening.

I am thinking of my mother is, of course, dedicated to my mother, Marcia Cope, and her habits of humorous and careful observation.

April Sunday Morning references Robert Lowell's "Blizzard in Cambridge," Wallace Stevens' "Sunday Morning," and Leroi Jones/Amiri Baraka's "Preface to a Twenty-Volume Suicide Note."

Blind is for Marike Finlay-de Monchy. I owe the phrase "trying to divine the true meaning and implications for the future – Deflation, Inflation, Devaluation, Armageddon" to an inspired post-2008 political rant by Paul Seamons. The story about being lost in the fog was based on several versions of the experience of being stranded near Stonington, Maine: thanks to Janice Stewart, Marike Finlay-de Monchy and Elisabeth Bigras for their accounts of that event.

When first you set out is dedicated to Blonde Sparrow, friend, artist, poet, and graceful survivor of catastrophe.

Acknowledgements

Not without the company and encouragement of poets, painters, artists, activists, fellow sailors, colleagues, students, family members, and friends, among them, for particular help, shelter, inspiration, or support as I've wrestled with portions of this manuscript: Carole Langille, Brian Cullen, Faizal Deen, Angella Parsons, Anne Simpson, Dee Vadnais, Paul Seamons, Rick and Dawn Burkmar, Chris Stockard, Barry Leonard, Max Haiven, Carla Taunton, Ericka Walker, Gary Markle, Steve Higgins, Jan Peacock, Alex Livingston, Heather MacLeod, Carole Bruneau, Mary MacLachlan, Jane Milton, Jayne Wark, Ken Rice, David Howard, Janice Stewart, Mary Bryson, Andy Parker, Bess Rose, Kristin Bergen, Susan Goldberg, Danica Meredith, Matt Bergbusch, Angel Beyde, Raphael Beaulieu, Marie-Therese Blanc, Jenn Maclatchy, Mar Molano, Peggy Cameron, Bill and Claire Williams, Liz McDougall, Ken Cheslock, Kevin Wilson, Karin Holland-Biggs, John Roston, Luke Carsons, Deb Esch, and Jean-François Bigras.

Not without Lesley Choyce, Julia Swan, and Peggy Amirault of Pottersfield Press who have made this book a reality; nor Paulette Phillips, who supplied both permission and a still from her *Floating House* video (2002) for the cover; nor the brilliant Raven Davis, who came up with a design solution for the cover, and Gail LeBlanc who executed the final version.

Not without my colleagues and co-workers at NSCAD and all of my students, above all not without their courage and unending generosity. Nor without the extraordinary help of so many remarkable librarians: Detta Morrison-Phillips, Kit Clarke, Jan Fralic-Brown, Rebecca Young, and Tanja Harrison and staff.

Not without dogs and cats and other creatures, including Binky, Bathsheba, Tiger, Linus, Dante, and now Enya, our Mexican rescue dog.

Not without my mother, Marcia Cope, who reads everything I send her, and my father, James Cope, who so often read us poetry. Not without my late maternal grandfather, Bill Smith's infernal silly rhymes – my first recollection of writing poems was of an afternoon with him. Nor without my siblings' equally droll love of wordplay.

Not without the sailboat *Quoddy's Run*, our access to so many of the places that appear in this work, nor without Blair and Sharon and Simon Fraser, who have made her better than new.

Nor ever without Elisabeth Bigras, elder, avid reader, culture hound, and wise co-voyager. She demonstrates daily how "delicious" living may be as she relishes sunlight and sudden flashes of fin or wing.

Above all, not without Marike Finlay-de Monchy, my collaborator in living, sailing, writing, being – if she didn't hear the words before I did, I'd never have written them down.

Author biography

Karin Cope divides her time between Nova Scotia and British Columbia. She is a poet, sailor, photographer, writer, activist, blogger, and Associate Professor at NSCAD University. Her publications include *Passionate Collaborations: Learning to Live with Gertrude Stein* and, since 2009, a photo/poetry blog entitled *Visible Poetry: Aesthetic Arts in Progress*: http://visiblepoetry.blogspot.com.